Miniature Quilts with Vintage Style

by Joyce Libal and the editors of *Miniature Quilts* magazine

CHITRA PUBLICATIONS

Chitra Publications
2 Public Avenue
Montrose, Pennsylvania 18801

First printing: 1999

Library of Congress Cataloging-in-Publication Data

Libal, Joyce.
Miniature quilts with vintage style / by Joyce Libal and
the editors of Miniature quilts magazine.
p.   cm.
ISBN 1-885588-28-3
1. Patchwork Patterns. 2. Miniature quilts. 3. Textile fabrics- -
Reproduction. I. Miniature quilts. II. Title.
TT835.L485   1999
746.46—dc21   99-30215
CIP

Edited by: Joyce Libal and Deborah Hearn
Design & Illustration: Kimberly A. Steele
Cover Photography: Guy Cali Associates, Clarks Summit, PA
Inside Photography: VanZandbergen Photography, Brackney, PA and
Stephen J. Appel, Vestal, NY

——— *Our Mission Statement* ———
We publish quality quilting magazines
and books that recognize, promote
and inspire self-expression.
We are dedicated to serving
our customers with respect,
kindness and efficiency.

$\mathcal{W}$elcome to Miniature Quilts with Vintage Style...

When I married and moved from my family home into my own home, I delighted in taking several treasured mementos with me. They were comforting to have around because each time I glanced at or touched them, they served as a reminder of happy times and special people. While stepping into the surprises and adventures that the future holds is exciting, it's also wonderful to bring our fondest memories along.

Just think—we're now at the dawn of the 21st-century! What that century holds for us as individuals, for our country and for the world remains to be seen. Undoubtedly, there will be huge advances in technology—perhaps even in the quilting tools and methods we use every day. What might a sewing machine look like and be able to do in the year 2035? We can only imagine, but I do believe that the quilts of the past will be even more valued in the future.

If you're like me, you'll want to take some of those quilts with you into your 21st-century adventure. The abundance of reproduction fabric available today makes it easy to create authentic, period-style quilts. And if you make minis, you don't have to stop at one. In no time, you can dress up your home with a collection of vintage-looking quilts.

Whether you live in the country or in a high-rise city apartment, there's nothing like a vignette of small but charming 20th-century quilts to warm your home. This collection was selected for you by the editors of *Miniature Quilts* magazine. Most of the quilts are made with 1930s-era reproduction fabrics. Look closely though and you may notice fabrics with looks that stretch back to the 1920s and "forward" to the 1940s. Quilts made with traditional blocks are included along with those that feature original designs. You'll even see prizewinners from our annual Miniatures from the Heart Contest! All of the patterns offer the easy stitching methods that *Miniature Quilts* is known for. So turn the pages and decide which quilts you're going to make. Then enjoy every moment you spend stitching and the new memories it builds.

Joyce Libal, Senior Editor
Miniature Quilts magazine

$\mathcal{C}$ontents

General Directions

Patterns

One Step at a Time

*Hot pink frames the
other bright colors
in this Jacob's Ladder.*

Years ago I made cloth dolls for each of my daughters. Angela and Autumn are now in college and their dolls have been sitting in a carriage for years waiting for a quilt of their own. It took a long time for me to get around to making **"One Step at a Time"** (19 1/2" square) for this purpose, but I think the traditional Jacob's Ladder was worth the wait.

QUILT SIZE: 19 1/2" square
BLOCK SIZE: 3" square

MATERIALS
Yardage is estimated for 44" fabric.
• Fat eighth (11" x 18") each of 8 bright prints
• 1/2 yard pink
• 2/3 yard muslin
• 1/2 yard green print
• 22" square of backing fabric
• 22" square of thin batting

CUTTING
Dimensions include a 1/4" seam allowance. Trim seams to 1/8" after stitching and pressing.
For the Jacob's Ladder blocks:
• Cut 16: 1" x 14" strips, 2 from each of the 8 bright prints
• Cut 1: 11" x 12 3/8" rectangle, muslin
• Cut 8: 1" x 14" strips, muslin
• Cut 2: 1" x 44" strips, muslin
• Cut 64: 1" squares, muslin
• Cut 2: 1" x 44" strips, pink
• Cut 1: 11" x 12 3/8" rectangle, pink
For the corner blocks:
• Cut 1: 1 1/2" x 8" strip, pink
• Cut 2: 1" x 15" strips, pink
• Cut 2: 1" x 8" strips, muslin
• Cut 1: 1 1/2" x 15" strip, muslin
For the inner pieced border:
• Cut 2: 1" x 44" strips, muslin
• Cut 4: 1" x 44" strips, green print
For the outer pieced border:
• Cut 96: 1" x 2 1/2" strips, assorted bright prints
• Cut 96: 1" squares, pink
Also:
• Cut 2: 1 3/4" x 44" strips, green print, for the binding

PREPARATION
• Mark a grid of 1 3/8" squares on the wrong side of the 11" x 12 3/8" muslin rectangle. Draw diagonal lines through the grid, as shown.

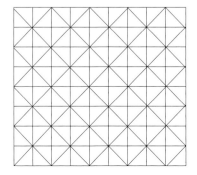

• Lay the marked rectangle on the 11" x 12 3/8" pink rectangle, right sides together, and sew 1/4" away from the diagonal lines on both sides. Cut the squares apart on the marked lines to yield 144 pieced squares. You will use 128.
NOTE*: Making the grid on a rectangle rather than a square allows you to stitch the grid in a continuous line.*

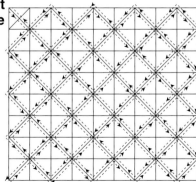

Start Here

DIRECTIONS
For the Jacob's Ladder blocks:
NOTE: *Two blocks will be made from each bright print.*
• Stitch a 1" x 14" muslin strip between two 1" x 14" matching bright print strips

to make a pieced panel, as shown. Make 8.

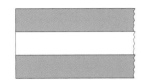

• Cut twelve 1" bright print slices from each pieced panel, as shown. Set them aside.

• Stitch a 1" x 44" muslin strip to a 1" x 44" pink strip to make a pieced strip. Make 2.
• From them cut sixty-four 1" pink pieced strips.

• Lay out 6 matching bright print slices, 8 pieced squares, 4 pink pieced strips and four 1" muslin squares in 6 rows, as shown.

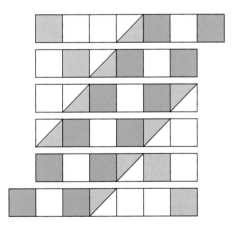

• Sew the strips and squares into rows.
• Remove the last square from the top row and the first square from the bottom row.
• Join the rows to make a Jacob's Ladder block Make 16.
• Referring to the quilt photo as needed, lay out the blocks in 4 rows of 4. Sew the blocks into rows and join the rows.

For the Corner blocks:
• Stitch a 1 1/2" x 8" pink strip between two 1" x 8" muslin strips to make a pieced panel.
• Cut four 1 1/2" slices from the pieced panel and label them A.
• Stitch a 1 1/2" x 15" muslin strip between two 1" x 15" pink strips to make a pieced panel.
• Cut eight 1" slices from the pieced panel and label them B.
• Stitch an A between two B's to make a corner block. Make 4. Set them aside.

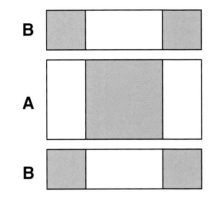

For the Inner Pieced border:
• Stitch a 1" x 44" muslin strip between two 1" x 44" green print strips, right sides together along their length, to form a pieced strip. Make 2.
• From each pieced strip, cut a 19 1/2" slice, a 12 1/2" slice and two 2 1/2" slices. Set them aside.

For the Outer Pieced border:
• Draw a diagonal line from corner to corner on the wrong side of each 1" pink square.
• Lay a marked pink square on a 1" x 2 1/2" bright print strip, right sides together, and sew on the drawn line, as shown.

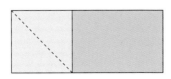

• Trim 1/8" beyond the seam. Open the unit and press the seam allowance toward the print. Make 96.

• Stitch 24 of the pieced units together to make an outer pieced border, as shown. Make 4.

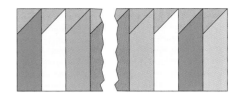

• Stitch outer pieced borders to two 12 1/2" inner pieced borders, as shown.

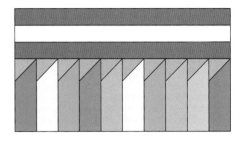

• Stitch them to opposite sides of the quilt.
• Stitch 2 corner blocks, two 2 1/2" inner pieced borders and an outer pieced border together to make a pieced unit, as shown. Make 2.

• Stitch a pieced unit to a 19 1/2" inner pieced border to make a pieced border section. Make 2.

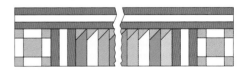

• Stitch the pieced border sections to the remaining sides of the quilt.
• Finish according to *Mini Stitching Tips*, using the 1 3/4" x 44" green print strips for the binding.

Around the Twist

Thread your favorite fabrics through interlocking rings.

Mary K. Richmond, of Santa Maria, California, has made three progressively smaller quilts in this design. She started with 3" blocks and ended with the 1 1/2" blocks of **"Around the Twist"** (17 1/2" x 20 1/2").

QUILT SIZE: 17 1/2" x 20 1/2"
BLOCK SIZE: 1 1/2" square

MATERIALS

Yardage is estimated for 44" fabric.
• Assorted print scraps, each at least 1 1/2" square
• 1/2 yard white
• Fat quarter (18" x 22") light blue print
• 20" x 23" piece of backing fabric
• 20" x 23" piece of thin batting

CUTTING

Dimensions include a 1/4" seam allowance.
NOTE: *Block A's each require four 1" x 1 1/2" print rectangles and one 1" white square. Block B's each require four 1 3/8" print squares and one 2" white square. The choice of prints for these pieces will be determined and cut as each block is made.*
• Cut 32: 1" squares, white
• Cut 31: 2" squares, white
• Cut 4: 1 1/4" x 15" strips, white
• Cut 4: 2 1/4" x 19" strips, white
• Cut 4: 1 1/4" x 17" strips, light blue print
• Cut 4: 1 3/4" x 22" strips, light blue print, for the binding

DIRECTIONS

NOTE: *Because of the interlocking design, it is necessary to select fabric for the print rectangles and squares, cut the pieces, lay out and stitch each block as you design the quilt on a flannel wall. Work on one block at a time, beginning with the top left corner. Complete each row before moving on to the next.*

For the first Block A:
• Cut and lay out four 1" x 1 1/2" print rectangles and a 1" white square, as shown.

• Stitch the 1" white square to the 1" x 1 1/2" top print rectangle, starting at one edge of the white square, and stopping at least 1/2" from the other edge of the white square, as shown.

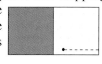

• Stitch the next rectangle to the white square and the short side of the first rectangle, as shown.

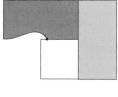

• In the same manner, sew the third and fourth print rectangles to the white square, as shown.

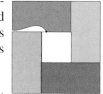

• Complete the first print rectangle's seam, joining it to the remainder of the white square and the fourth print rectangle, to finish the first Block A.

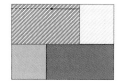

For the first Block B:
• Working off of the first Block A, lay out a 2" white square and cut four 1 3/8" print squares, being sure the prints for the left side of Block B match the appropriate prints used in the first Block A, to begin forming the interlocking design. Refer to the Assembly Diagram and the color photo, as needed.
• Fold each 1 3/8" print square in half diagonally, wrong sides together, to form a triangle. Finger press along the fold.

- Place the folded triangles in the appropriate corners of the 2" white square.
- Open the folded triangles, keeping them in the correct corners and pin them, right sides together, to the 2" white square. Stitch along the pressed line of the first print square, as shown.

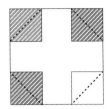

- In the same manner, stitch along the pressed line of the remaining 3 print squares. To complete a block B, trim the seam allowances beyond each stitching line, open the corners and press the seam allowances toward the print.

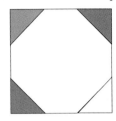

- Cut and lay out the pieces for the second Block A, referring to the first Block B for appropriate color selection. Stitch the pieces together in the same manner as before.

- Continue working across the row until 4 Block A's and 3 Block B's are complete. Stitch the blocks into a horizontal row.
- Start row #2 with a Block B by laying out a 2" white square and cutting four 1 3/8" print squares that coordinate with the Block A and Block B above it. Stitch the block together, as before.
- Stitch a total of 4 Block B's and 3 Block A's, being careful to coordinate the prints to adjacent blocks, to create the interlocking design.
- Stitch the row 2 blocks together.
- In the same manner, make blocks for a total of 9 rows. Join the rows.
- Measure length of the quilt. Trim 2 of the 1 1/4" x 15" white strips to that measurement and stitch them to the long sides of the quilt.
- Measure the width of the quilt, including the borders. Trim the remaining 1 1/4" x 15" white strips to that measurement and stitch them to the remaining sides of the quilt.
- In the same manner, trim 2 of the 1 1/4" x 17" light blue print strips to fit the quilt's length and stitch them to the long sides of the quilt.
- Trim the remaining 1 1/4" x 17" light blue print strips, and stitch them to the remaining sides of the quilt.
- Trim 2 of the 2 1/4" x 19" white

strips and stitch them to the long sides of the quilt.
- Trim the remaining 2 1/4" x 19" white strips, and stitch them to the remaining sides of the quilt.
- Finish according to *Mini Stitching Tips*, using the 1 3/4" x 22" light blue print strips for the binding.

ASSEMBLY DIAGRAM

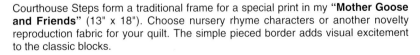

Mother Goose and Friends

Framed nursery tale friends make a delightful miniature

Courthouse Steps form a traditional frame for a special print in my **"Mother Goose and Friends"** (13" x 18"). Choose nursery rhyme characters or another novelty reproduction fabric for your quilt. The simple pieced border adds visual excitement to the classic blocks.

QUILT SIZE: 13" x 18"
BLOCK SIZE: 4 1/2" square

MATERIALS
Yardage is estimated for 44" fabric.
- 6 scraps of red print with

Mother Goose motifs, each at least 2" square
- Assorted red print and solid scraps, each at least 1 1/4" square
- Assorted black print scraps, each at least 1 1/4" square
- Fat quarter (18" x 22") black

- Fat eighth (11" x 18") light plaid
- Fat eighth black print
- Fat eighth second black print
- Fat eighth white print
- Fat eighth muslin
- 15" x 20" piece of backing fabric
- 15" x 20" piece of thin batting

CUTTING

Dimensions include a 1/4" seam allowance. Trim seams to 1/8" after stitching and pressing.

For the blocks:

- Cut 6: 2" squares, Mother Goose print, with a motif centered in each square
- Cut 12: 1" x 2" strips, light plaid
- Cut 12: 1" x 3" strips, first black print
- Cut 12: 1" x 3" strips, white print
- Cut 12: 1" x 4" strips, black
- Cut 12: 1" x 4" strips, muslin
- Cut 12: 1" x 5" strips, second black print

For the pieced border:

- Cut 56: 1 1/4" squares, black and assorted black prints
- Cut 56: 1 1/4" squares, assorted muslin and light plaid
- Cut 56: 1 1/4" squares, red and assorted red prints

Also:

- Cut 3: 1" x 5" strips, black, for the sashings
- Cut 4: 1" x 10 1/2" strips, black, for the sashings
- Cut 2: 1" x 16" strips, black
- Cut 4: 1 1/2" squares, black
- Cut 4: 1 3/4" x 22" strips, black, for the binding

DIRECTIONS

For each of the 6 blocks:

- Stitch 1" x 2" light plaid strips to the left and right sides of a Mother Goose square. Press the seam allowance away from the center square.

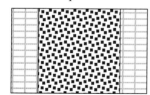

- Stitch 1" x 3" first black print strips to the top and bottom of the Mother Goose unit. Press the seam allowance away from the center square.
- In the same man-

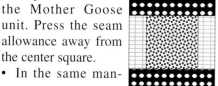

ner, stitch 1" x 3" white print strips to the left and right sides of the unit. Stitch 1" x 4" black strips to the top and bottom of the unit.
- Stitch 1" x 4" muslin strips to the left and right sides of the unit. Stitch 1" x 5" second black print strips to the top and bottom of the unit to complete the block.

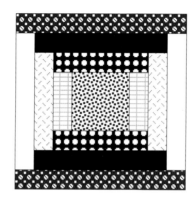

ASSEMBLY

- Stitch a 1" x 5" black strip between 2 blocks to complete a row. Make 3.
- Lay out the rows with a 1" x 10 1/2" black strip between them and at the top and bottom of the quilt.

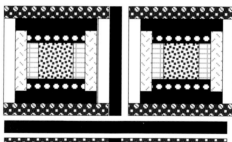

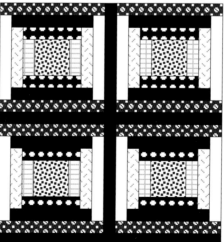

- Stitch the rows and strips together.
- Stitch 1" x 16" black strips to the left and right sides of the quilt.

For the pieced border:

- Lay out a 1 1/4" black print or black square, a 1 1/4" muslin or light plaid square, and a 1 1/4" red print or red square, as shown. Stitch them together to form a border unit. Make 56.

- Join 12 border units, offsetting the units as shown, to make a short border. Make 2.

- Measure the width of the quilt and trim the short borders to that measurement, trimming units on both ends, as shown.

- Trim the long edges of the short borders, leaving a 1/4" seam allowance beyond the points of the muslin squares, as shown. Set the borders aside.

- In the same manner, stitch 16 border units together to make a long border. Make 2.
- Measure the length of the quilt and trim the long borders to that measurement.
- Trim the long edges of the borders, as before.
- Stitch a 2" black square to each short end of a long border. Make 2.

- Referring to the quilt photo, stitch the short borders to the top and bottom of the quilt.
- Stitch the long borders to the sides of the quilt.
- Finish according to the *Mini Stitching Tips,* using the 1 3/4" x 22" black strips for the binding.

Mom, I'll Always Remember

Make a quilt of unforgettable quotes to honor someone special.

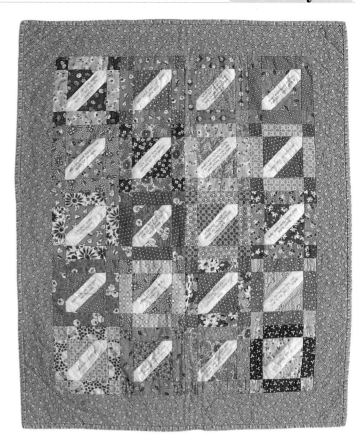

"Mom, I'll Always Remember" (25" x 30") is a touching tribute by Jan Winters of Memphis, Tennessee, for her mother. In her quilt, Jan included vintage prints which belonged to her grandmother and great-grandmother. She was inspired to print the "mom quotes" because she's a mother herself and has used many of these lines on her own children. "I wasn't born yesterday!", "Because I said so" and "I Love You" are just a few. Do they sound familiar? The Chitra Publications staff also enjoyed a comment Jan made on the Quilt Questionnaire she completed, "Mirror, mirror on the wall, I'm like my mother after all." ☺

QUILT SIZE: 25" x 30"
BLOCK SIZE: 5" square

MATERIALS
Yardage is estimated for 44" fabric.
- 40 bright prints, each at least 4" x 6 1/2"
- 1/4 yard muslin
- 3/8 yard pink print for the border
- 1/4 yard green print for the binding
- 27" x 32" piece of backing fabric
- 27" x 32" piece of thin batting
- Fine tip permanent marker

CUTTING
For each of 20 blocks:
NOTE: *Pair 2 contrasting prints for each block.*
- Cut 4: 1 1/2" squares, one print
- Cut 1: 3 1/8" square, same print, then cut it in half diagonally to yield 2 triangles
- Cut 4: 1 1/2" x 3 1/2" strips, contrasting print
Also:
- Cut 20: 1 1/2" x 5 1/4" strips, muslin
- Cut 4: 2 3/4" x 27" strips, pink print, for the border
- Cut 3: 1 3/4" x 44" strips, green print, for the binding

DIRECTIONS
For each of 20 blocks:
- Fold each print triangle in half and

crease to mark the center. Fold a 1 1/2" x 5 1/4" muslin strip in half and mark the center in the same manner.
- Stitch a print triangle to one side of the muslin strip, right sides together and aligning the center creases.
- Repeat, stitching the remaining triangle to the opposite side of the muslin strip to make a block center. Press the seam allowances toward the triangles. Trim the corners of the muslin strip to square the unit. Set it aside.
- Stitch a 1 1/2" same print square to each end of a 1 1/2" x 3 1/2" contrasting print strip to make a pieced strip. Make 2.

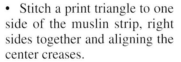

- Lay out the block center, the remaining 1 1/2" x 3 1/2" contrasting print strips and the pieced strips, as shown.

- Join them to make a block.
- Using a fine tip permanent marker, write a favorite saying on the muslin strip of each block. (See the quotes Jan used for her quilt on page 29. Also see the Quiltmaker's tip below.)

ASSEMBLY
- Referring to the photo, lay out the blocks in 5 rows of 4. Stitch the blocks into rows. Join the rows.
- Measure the length of the quilt. Trim 2 of the 2 3/4" x 27" pink print strips to that measurement. Stitch them to the sides of the quilt.
- Measure the width of the quilt, including the borders. Trim the remaining 2 3/4" x 27" pink print strips to that measurement Stitch them to the top and bottom of the quilt.
- Finish according to *Mini Stitching Tips,* using the 1 3/4" x 44" green print strips for the binding.

Quiltermaker's Tip:
Jan printed her quotes on the computer, then transferred them to muslin via copy machine. You can do the same, but be sure the text area is no larger than 3/4" x 3". This allows for a little space around the text when the block is sewn. Cut out a 1 1/2" x 5 1/4" muslin strip for each block, centering the quote on the strip.

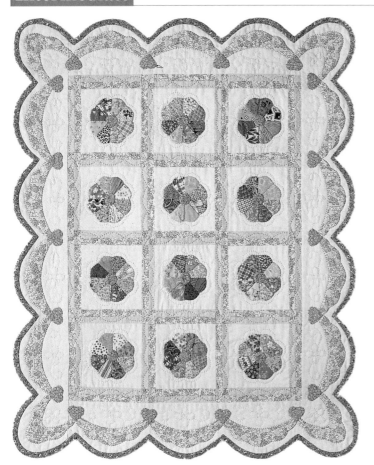

Dresden Charms

An appliqué beauty like this is destined to become a treasured heirloom.

"Dresden Charms" (20" x 24 1/4") by Susan Holman, of Laytonsville, Maryland, won First Place in the Traditional Appliqué category of the 1994 Miniatures from the Heart Contest.

QUILT SIZE: 20" x 24 1/4"
BLOCK SIZE: 3 1/2" square

MATERIALS
Yardage is estimated for 44" fabric.
- Assorted pastel print and solid scraps, each at least 1 1/2" square
- 1/2 yard cream
- 1/8 yard light blue print
- 1/4 yard pale pink print
- 1/4 yard yellow print
- 1/4 yard green print
- 1/8 yard pink print
- 1/2 yard blue print, for the binding
- 22" x 27" piece of backing fabric
- 22" x 27" piece of thin batting
- Freezer paper

CUTTING
Appliqué pattern pieces A through E are full size and do not include a seam allowance. Trace the specified number of pattern pieces on freezer paper and cut them out on the traced lines. Iron the freezer paper templates to the wrong side of the fabric. When cutting each piece, add a 1/8" turn-under allowance. Do not remove the freezer paper. All other dimensions include a 1/4" seam allowance.
- Cut 96: A, assorted pastel prints and solids
- Cut 12: B, light blue print
- Cut 4: C, green print
- Cut 14: D, green print
- Cut 18: E, pink print
- Cut 4: 7/8" x 44" strips, pale pink print, for the sashing
- Cut 4: 7/8" x 44" strips, yellow print, for the sashing
- Cut 12: 4" squares, cream
- Cut 2: 3 1/2" x 19" strips, cream
- Cut 2: 3 1/2" x 21" strips, cream
- Cut 1 1/2"-wide bias strips, blue print, to equal 110" in length, for the binding

DIRECTIONS
- Stitch 2 A's right sides together along the edge of the freezer paper templates. Press the seam allowance to the left, leaving the freezer paper in place. Make 48 pairs.
- Join 2 pairs to make half of a Dresden Plate. Press the seam allowance in the same direction. Make 24.
- Join 2 halves to make a Dresden Plate. Press the seam allowances in the same direction as before. Make 12.

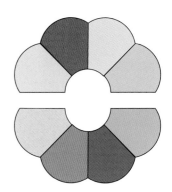

- Carefully press the outer edge of each Dresden Plate over the edge of the freezer paper templates. Remove the freezer paper. Center and pin a Dresden Plate on a 4" cream square. Appliqué the plate in place. Make 12.
- In the same way, press the turn-under allowance for each B. Remove the freezer paper templates. Appliqué a B in the center of each block, covering the inner raw edges of the Dresden Plate. Make 12.
- Press the Dresden Plate blocks lightly from the wrong side.
- Stitch a 7/8" x 44" pale pink print strip to a 7/8" x 44" yellow print strip, right sides together along their length. Make 4 pieced strips.
- Cut the pieced strips into thirty-one

4" slices for sashing strips and forty 7/8" slices for Four Patch cornerstones, as shown.

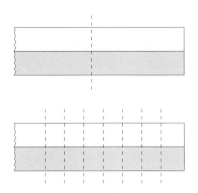

A

E

B

C

D

• Join two 7/8" slices to make a cornerstone. Make 20.
• Lay out the Dresden Plate blocks, the 4" sashing strips and the Four Patches, referring to the Assembly Diagram.

• Stitch them into rows. Join the rows.

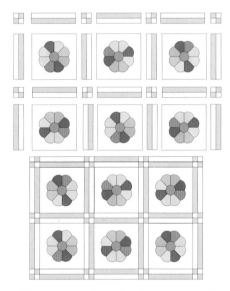

• Measure the length of the quilt. Trim the 3 1/2" x 19" cream strips to that measurement. Stitch them to the long sides of the quilt.
• Measure the width of the quilt, including the borders. Trim the 3 1/2" x 20" cream strips to that measurement. Stitch them to the remaining sides of the quilt.
• Prepare the C, D and E pieces for appliqué in the same manner as the A and B pieces. Position and pin the D's on the cream border, spacing them 1 1/2" from the sashing border to the center of the D swags. Make sure the D swags are directly across from the Dresden Plate blocks. Position and pin

the C's on the cream border, spacing them 2" from the sashing corner to the center of the C swags. Appliqué them in place.
• Appliqué an E at the ends of each swag.
• Draw a line 1/2" from the outside edge of the swags, forming scallops. The corner scallops will be narrower to mimic the shape of the corner swags. Do not cut along this line.
• Layer and baste the backing, batting and quilt top according to *Mini Stitching Tips*.
• Baste 1/4" inside the marked line on the quilt.
• Stitch the 1 1/2" bias binding strips together with diagonal seams; trim and press the seams open. Press a short end of the bias strip under 1/4" to make the starting end.

• Fold one long edge of the binding strip, 1/4" toward the wrong side and press.
• Lay the binding on the top of the quilt right sides together. Align the raw edge of the binding with the drawn line of the scallops, beginning in the middle of a curved drawn line. The pressed edge of the binding will be toward the center of the quilt. Begin stitching 1/4" from the folded end.

NOTE: *You may wish to pin the binding*

to the quilt at each scallop as you are working on it.
• Stitch the binding, being careful not to stretch it as you sew. When approaching an inside corner, stop with needle in the quilt and lift the presser foot. Pivot your quilt, repositioning the binding. Lower the presser foot and continue stitching 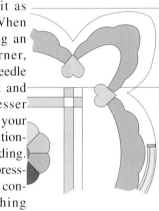 the next scallop. On the corner scallops, ease in the fullness of the binding.
• Stitch all the way around, stopping 1" from the start of the binding.
• Overlap the ends of the binding and trim the excess 1/4" past the beginning of the binding.
• Stitch the ends of the binding together with a 1/4" seam.
• Finish stitching the binding to the quilt.
• Trim the edges of the quilt top, batting and backing along the marked line.
• Turn the binding to the back of the quilt and blindstitch the folded edge in place.

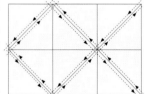

Spring Baskets

Embellish your quilt with embroidered flora and fauna.

A full-size antique quilt featured in *Traditional Quiltworks* magazine provided the inspiration for **Spring Baskets** (12 1/2" square). I loved the chunky handles and over-sized embroidery motifs on the antique and decided to incorporate those elements in a miniature. Making this little quilt will warm your heart, even on the coldest winter day.

QUILT SIZE: 12 1/2" square
BLOCK SIZE: 3" square

MATERIALS

Yardage is estimated for 44" fabric.
- Fat quarter (18" x 22") turquoise print
- Fat eighth (11" x 18") pink print
- Fat eighth muslin
- 15" square of backing fabric
- 15" square of thin batting
- Embroidery floss: dark and light green, turquoise, purple, pink, rust and yellow

CUTTING

Dimensions include a 1/4" seam allowance. Trim seams to 1/8" after stitching and pressing.
- Cut 2: 4 1/4" squares, pink print
- Cut 2: 3/4" x 4 1/2" bias strips, pink print
- Cut 6: 1 3/8" squares, pink print, then cut them in half diagonally to yield 12 triangles
- Cut 1: 3" x 4 1/2" rectangle, pink print
- Cut 4: 1 3/4" x 18" strips, pink print, for the binding
- Cut 2: 4 1/4" squares, turquoise print
- Cut 2: 3/4" x 4 1/2" bias strips, turquoise print
- Cut 6: 1 3/8" squares, turquoise print, then cut them in half diagonally to yield 12 triangles
- Cut 1: 3" x 4 1/2" rectangle, turquoise print
- Cut 4: 3/4" x 3" strips, turquoise print
- Cut 8: 1" x 9 1/2" strips, turquoise print
- Cut 2: 1" x 5" strips, turquoise print
- Cut 1: 1" x 9" strip, turquoise print
- Cut 2: 3" x 4 1/2" rectangles, muslin
- Cut 1: 3" square, muslin
- Cut 4: 3/4" squares, muslin
- Cut 4: 1" x 9 1/2" strips, muslin
- Cut 2: 1 7/8" squares, muslin, then cut them in half diagonally to yield 4 medium triangles
- Cut 2: 3 7/8" squares, muslin, then cut them in half diagonally to yield 4 large triangles
- Cut 1: 1" x 5" strip, muslin
- Cut 2: 1" x 9" strips, muslin
- Cut 8: 1" x 2 1/2" strips, muslin

PREPARATION
- Mark a grid of 1 1/2" squares on the wrong side of each 3" x 4 1/2" muslin rectangle, as shown.
- Mark diagonal

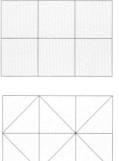

lines through the intersections on the grid, as shown.
- Lay a marked muslin rectangle on a 3" x 4 1/2" pink print rectangle, right sides together, and sew 1/4" away from the diagonal lines on both sides.
- Cut the squares apart on the marked lines to yield 12 pink pieced squares. Trim them to 1" square.
- In the same manner, lay a marked muslin rectangle on a 3" x 4 1/2" turquoise print rectangle and sew 1/4" away from the diagonal lines on both sides. Cut as before to yield 12 turquoise pieced squares. Trim them to 1" square.

PIECING
- Sew 2 of the 3/4" x 3" turquoise print strips to opposite sides of the 3" muslin square.
- Sew a 3/4" muslin square to each short end of the remaining 3/4" x 3" turquoise print strips.
- Sew them to the remaining sides of the muslin square to complete the cen-

ter block. Set it aside.

• Draw diagonal lines from corner to corner on the wrong side of each 4 1/4" turquoise print square.

• Lay a marked turquoise print square on a 4 1/4" pink print square, right sides together, and sew 1/4" away from one of the drawn lines on both sides, as shown. Make 2.

• Cut the squares apart on the drawn lines to yield 8 pieced triangles.

• Sew 2 pieced triangles together, as shown, to complete a setting block. Make 4. Set them aside.

• Remembering to leave a 1/4" seam allowance on all sides, lightly mark the placement of the basket handle on each of the 4 large muslin triangles.

• Trace a different floral embroidery motif beneath the handle marking in each muslin triangle. Trace the bird embroidery motif in the center block.

• Turn under a 1/4" seam allowance along the long edges of both 3/4" x 4 1/2" pink print bias strips and press. Trim each pressed edge to 1/8". Appliqué them in place to complete 2 pink handle units. Set them aside.

• In the same manner, turn under a 1/4" seam allowance along the long edges of the 3/4" x 4 1/2" turquoise print bias strips. Press, trim and appliqué them to the 2 remaining muslin triangles. Set them aside.

• Lay out 5 turquoise pieced squares, 1 pink pieced square and 4 turquoise triangles in 4 rows, as shown.

• Sew the squares and triangles into rows and join the rows to complete a basket triangle. Make 2 turquoise basket triangles. In the same manner, make 2 pink basket triangles.

• Sew a pink triangle to a short end of a 1" x 2 1/2" muslin strip. Repeat, alternating the

direction of the triangle, as shown. Make 2 of each unit. In the same manner, sew turquoise triangles to one short end of the 4 remaining 1" x 2 1/2" muslin strips, alternating the direction of the triangles, as before.

• Sew the strips with pink triangles to opposite sides of the turquoise basket triangles. Sew the strips with turquoise triangles to opposite sides of the pink basket triangles.

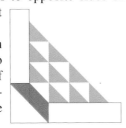

• Sew a medium muslin triangle to the bottom of each basket triangle to complete the basket units.

• Sew pink handle units to the turquoise basket units, and turquoise handle units to the pink basket units to complete the 4 basket blocks. Trim the excess from the muslin side strips, as shown.

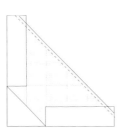

• Referring to the quilt photo as needed, lay out the blocks in 3 rows of 3, placing each setting block so that a pink triangle is touching the center block. Sew the blocks into rows and join the rows.

• Sew a 1" x 9" turquoise print strip between two 1" x 9" muslin strips, along

their length, to form a pieced strip.

• Cut eight 1" slices from the pieced strip.

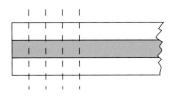

• In the same manner, sew a 1" x 5" muslin strip between two 1" x 5" turquoise print strips. Cut four 1" slices from the pieced strip.

• Sew 2 slices with turquoise print centers and 1 slice with a muslin center together to complete a Nine Patch block. Make 4. Set them aside.

• Sew a 1" x 9 1/2" muslin strip between two 1" x 9 1/2" turquoise print strips, along their length, to form a pieced border. Make 4.

• Sew a pieced border to 2 opposite sides of the quilt.

• Sew a Nine Patch block to each end of the 2 remaining pieced borders.

• Sew them to the remaining sides of the quilt.

• Referring to the quilt photo as needed, embroider the motifs, using a satin stitch, outline stitch and French knots. (Directions for French knots are on page 18.)

• Finish according to *Mini Stitching Tips*, using the 1 3/4" x 18" pink print strips for the binding.

Grandmother's Choice Doll Quilt

© by Lisa W. Benson

Make a nostalgic scrap quilt with an authentic look of yesteryear.

"Grandmother's Choice Doll Quilt" (17 1/4" x 21 3/4") by Lisa W. Benson of Erie, Pennsylvania, was inspired by an antique. Lisa explains, "I saw an antique doll quilt in this pattern at a quilt show and decided to make my own!" The resulting quilt is wonderful.

QUILT SIZE: 17 1/4" x 21 3/4"
BLOCK SIZE: 3 1/8" square

MATERIALS
Yardage is estimated for 44" fabric.
- 12 print scraps, each at least 4" x 7"
- 1/2 yard muslin
- 1/3 yard yellow print
- 1/4 yard second yellow print, for the binding
- 20" x 24" piece of backing fabric
- 20" x 24" piece of thin batting

CUTTING
All dimensions include a 1/4" seam allowance.
For each of 12 blocks:
- Cut 5: 1 1/8" squares, print scrap. Label them A.
- Cut 2: 2 1/8" squares, same print scrap, then cut them in half diagonally to yield 4 triangles. Label them B.
Also:
- Cut 48: 1 1/2" squares, muslin, then cut them in half diagonally to yield 96 triangles. Label them C.
- Cut 48: 1 1/8" x 1 3/4" rectangles, muslin. Label them D.
- Cut 6: 3 5/8" squares, muslin

- Cut 3: 5 3/4" squares, muslin, then cut them in quarters diagonally to yield 12 setting triangles. You will use 10.
- Cut 2: 3 1/8" squares, muslin, then cut them in half diagonally to yield 4 corner triangles
- Cut 4: 2 1/4" x 24" strips, yellow print, for the border
- Cut 3: 1 3/4" x 32" strips, second yellow print, for the binding

DIRECTIONS
For each of 12 blocks:
- Stitch 2 C's to adjacent sides of an A, to make a pieced triangle. Stitch a B to a pieced triangle to make a pieced square. Make 4.

ASSEMBLY DIAGRAM

14

• Stitch a D between 2 pieced squares to make a pieced unit. Make 2.

• Stitch an A between 2 D's to make a pieced strip.

• Lay out the pieced units and pieced strip, as shown. Join the rows to complete a block.

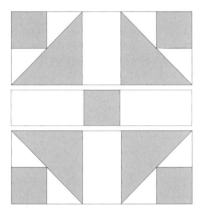

ASSEMBLY

• Lay out the blocks, the 3 5/8" muslin squares and the setting and corner triangles, as shown in the Assembly Diagram. Stitch them into diagonal rows. Join the rows.

• Measure the length of the quilt. Trim 2 of the 2 1/4" x 24" yellow print strips to that measurement. Stitch them to the long sides of the quilt.

• Measure the width of the quilt, including the borders. Trim the remaining 2 1/4" x 24" yellow print strips to that measurement. Stitch them to the remaining sides of the quilt.

• Finish according to *Mini Stitching Tips,* using the 1 3/4" x 32" second yellow print strips for the binding.

Vintage Tumbler Charm

Stitch a quilt that's charmingly pieced with small scraps.

Diane Albeck-Grick, the art director for *Miniature Quilts* magazine, stitched **"Vintage Tumbler Charm"** (20 1/2" x 22 1/2") to showcase a collection of vintage fabrics. Whether made from vintage fabrics or reproduction prints, the simple Tumbler unit is an excellent choice for a charm quilt. Fussy cut your favorite prints (like Diane did for the sailor and her puppy units) to make your quilt even more delightful.

QUILT SIZE: 20 1/2" x 22 1/2"

MATERIALS
Yardage is estimated for 44" fabric.
• 110 assorted print scraps, each at least 3" square
• 1/4 yard blue print, for the binding
• 23" x 25" piece of backing fabric
• 23" x 25" piece of thin batting

CUTTING
All dimensions include a 1/4" seam allowance.
• Cut 110: A, print scraps

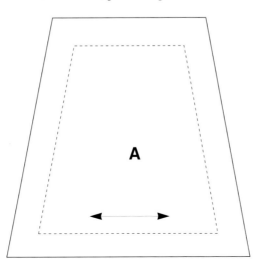

• Cut 3: 1 3/4" x 44" strips, blue print, for the binding.

DIRECTIONS
• Lay out the A's in 11 rows of 10, arranging the fabrics in a layout that pleases you, and referring to the photo as necessary.
• Stitch the A's into rows and join the rows.
• Trim to straighten the uneven edges of the quilt, as shown.

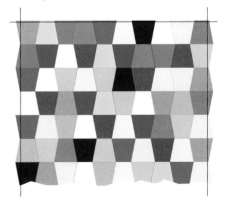

• Finish according to *Mini Stitching Tips,* using the 1 3/4" x 44" blue print strips for the binding.

Petite Sunbonnet Sue

It's easy with fusible appliqué!

As the art director for *Miniature Quilts* magazine, Diane Albeck-Grick found inspiration for her "**Petite Sunbonnet Sue**" (15" x 18") in a note sent in by a reader. The reader had made a Sunbonnet Sue quilt in 1930's-style reproduction fabric. Upon hearing that, Diane thought such a quilt would be a great resting place for some of the vintage fabric she had collected. It must be summer in Diane's quilt as her thumb print sized Sue appears to be wearing a sunsuit. That's why you can see her knees.

QUILT SIZE: 15" x 18"
BLOCK SIZE: 2 1/2" square

MATERIALS
Yardage is estimated for 44" fabric
• Assorted scraps in lights, mediums and darks, each at least 1 1/4" square, for the dresses and hats
• 1/4 yard muslin
• 1/8 yard first pink print
• 1/8 yard second pink print
• 1/8 yard burgundy print
• 17" x 20" piece of backing fabric
• 17" x 20" piece of thin batting
• Fusible web
• Black embroidery floss

CUTTING
Fusible appliqué pieces are full-size and do not need a seam allowance. All other dimensions include a 1/4" seam allowance.
• Cut 20: 3" squares, muslin, for the background
• Cut 15: 1" x 3" strips, first pink print, for the sashing
• Cut 4: 1" x 12" strips, first pink print, for the sashing
• Cut 2: 2" x 13" strips, second pink print, for the border
• Cut 2: 2" x 19" strips, second pink print, for the border
• Cut 2: 1 3/4" x 44" strips, burgundy print, for the binding

DIRECTIONS
• Trace the dress and hat, 20 times each, on the paper side of the fusible web. Cut them out slightly beyond the drawn line.
• Following the manufacturer's directions, adhere the pieces to the wrong side of the assorted scraps. Cut them out on the drawn lines.
• Remove the paper backing, center and press the dresses and hats in place on the 3" muslin squares.

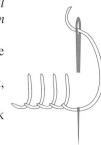

• Using one or two strands of black embroidery floss, work a blanket stitch around the dresses and hats. Use a straight stitch for the legs, referring to the quilt photo for positioning ideas.
• Lay out the blocks, 1" x 3" first pink print sashing strips and 1" x 12" first pink print sashing strips, referring to the photo, as necessary.
• Stitch the blocks and short sashing strips into horizontal rows.
• Join the rows and long sashing strips.
• Measure the width of the quilt. Trim the 2" x 13" second pink print strips to that measurement. Stitch them to the top and bottom of the quilt.
• Measure the length of the quilt, including the borders. Trim the 2" x 19" second pink print strips to that measurement. Stitch them to the sides of the quilt.

hat

dress

• Finish according to *Mini Stitching Tips,* using the 1 3/4" x 44" burgundy print strips for the binding.

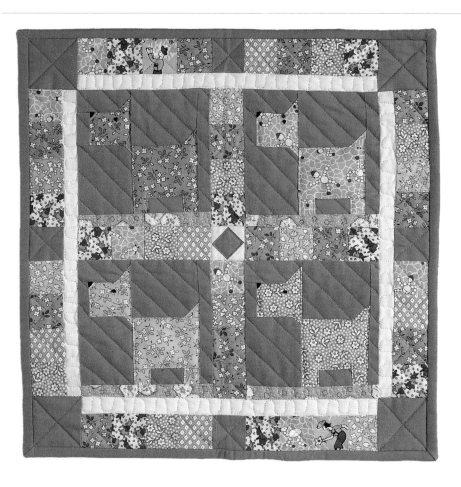

Scottie Dogs

*Create perky pups
without set-in seams
or curved piecing.*

Ever since reading about President Franklin Roosevelt's dog, Fala, I've wanted to make a Scottie dog quilt. After having difficulty locating a traditional block without curved seams, I decided to design my own for **"Scottie Dogs"** (12 1/2" square). Wouldn't these pups be the perfect "guard dogs" for a child's nursery?

QUILT SIZE: 12 1/2" square
BLOCK SIZE: 4" square

MATERIALS
Yardage is estimated for 44" fabric.
• Fat quarter (18" x 22") blue
• 4 print scraps, each at least 5" square
• Assorted print scraps, each at least 1 1/2" square
• Fat eighth (11" x 18") muslin
• 15" square of backing fabric
• 15" square of thin batting
• Black embroidery floss

CUTTING
Dimensions include a 1/4" seam allowance. Trim seams to 1/8" after stitching and pressing.
For each of 4 blocks:
• Cut 1: 1 1/2" x 1 3/4" rectangle, print
• Cut 1: 2 1/8" x 2 1/2" rectangle, matching print
• Cut 2: 1" squares, matching print
• Cut 3: 7/8" squares, matching print
Also:
• Cut 4: 1" x 2 1/8" rectangles, blue
• Cut 4: 2" x 2 1/2" rectangles, blue
• Cut 4: 7/8" x 4 1/8" strips, blue

• Cut 4: 1" x 1 1/2" rectangles, blue
• Cut 4: 2 1/8" x 2 5/8" rectangles, blue
• Cut 4: 7/8" x 1 1/2" rectangles, blue
• Cut 1: 1 1/8" square, blue
• Cut 4: 2" squares, blue
• Cut 4: 1 1/2" squares, blue
• Cut 4: 1 3/4" x 18" strips, blue, for the binding
• Cut 4: 7/8" x 4 1/2" strips, green print
• Cut 2: 1 5/8" squares, muslin, then cut them in half diagonally to yield 4 triangles
• Cut 4: 1" x 9 1/2" strips, muslin
• Cut 48: 1 1/2" squares, assorted print scraps

DIRECTIONS
• Draw a diagonal line from corner to corner on the wrong side of each 7/8" print square.
• Lay a marked square on a 1" x 2 1/8" blue rectangle, right sides together, and stitch on the marked line, as shown.

• Open the unit and press the seam allowance toward the blue. Trim the same allowance to 1/8" beyond the seam to complete the ear unit.
• Lay a marked square on a 2 1/8" x 2 5/8" blue rectangle, right sides together, and stitch on the marked line, as shown.

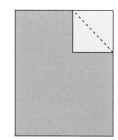

• Trim and press to complete the neck unit.
• Lay a marked square on a 2" x 2 1/2" blue rectangle, right sides together, and stitch on the marked line, as shown.

- Trim and press to complete the tail unit.
- Stitch a 1" x 1 1/2" blue rectangle between 2 matching 1" print squares to complete a leg unit.

- Stitch the leg unit to the 2 1/8" x 2 1/2" matching print rectangle.

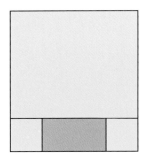

- Stitch a 7/8" x 1 1/2" blue rectangle to a 1 1/2" x 1 3/4" matching print rectangle to complete a head unit.

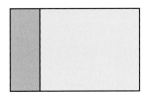

- Stitch the ear unit to the head unit.

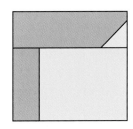

- Lay out the head, neck, tail and leg units, as shown.

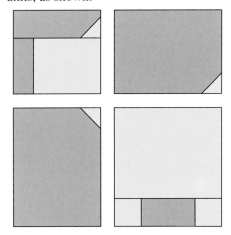

- Stitch them into 2 rows and join the rows to make a Scottie unit.

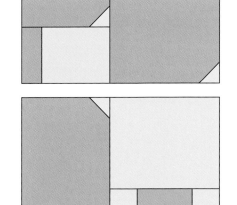

- Stitch a 7/8" x 4 1/8" blue strip to the right side of the Scottie Unit. Stitch a 7/8" x 4 1/2" green print strip to the bottom to complete a Scottie block. Make 4. Set them aside.

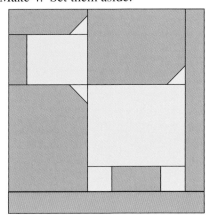

- Stitch muslin triangles to opposite sides of the 1 1/8" blue square.

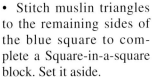

- Stitch muslin triangles to the remaining sides of the blue square to complete a Square-in-a-square block. Set it aside.

- Stitch four 1 1/2" print squares together to form a pieced strip. Make 12.
- Stitch the Square-in-a-square block between 2 pieced strips to complete the sashing strip.

ASSEMBLY
- Referring to the quilt photo as needed, lay out 2 rows of 2 blocks, with a pieced strip between the blocks, and the sashing strip between the rows.
- Stitch the blocks and vertical pieced strips into rows. Join the rows and sashing strip.
- Stitch a 1 1/2" blue square between 2 pieced strips to make a pieced border. Make 4.
- Stitch a 1" x 9 1/2" muslin strip to each pieced border.

- Stitch 2 of the pieced borders to opposite sides of the quilt, keeping the muslin strip against the quilt.
- Stitch a 2" blue square to each end of the remaining pieced borders.
- Stitch them to the remaining sides of the quilt, keeping the muslin strip against the quilt.
- Referring to the quilt photo as needed, embroider the dogs' noses with a satin stitch and the eyes with a French knot.
- Finish according to *Mini Stitching Tips*, using the 1 3/4" x 18" blue strips for the binding.

French Knots
- Thread a needle with three strands of embroidery floss. Knot one end and pull the needle from the back of the quilt top through the fabric at the exact point that you wish the dog's eye to appear.
- Holding the needle in your right hand, pull the thread taught with your left hand. Keeping the needle close to the fabric, wrap the thread around the needle four times.
- Keeping the wrapped thread near the tip of the needle, reinsert the needle into the fabric just beside its exit point.
- Gently pull the needle through to the back of the quilt top, making sure the knot remains close to the fabric.
- Knot off the thread on the back of the quilt top.

Beggar's Blocks

Piece a sweet quilt with even your smallest scraps.

After buying an old green cradle with tiny daisies painted on it, Judy Peters wanted to make an accompanying quilt. The Rockford, Illinois, quilter chose a delightful assortment of fabrics to give **"Beggar's Blocks"** (8 1/2" x 11 1/2") it's cheerful look.

QUILT SIZE: 8 1/2" x 11 1/2"
BLOCK SIZE: 1 1/2" square

MATERIALS

Yardage is estimated for 44" fabric.
• 35 assorted scraps of light and medium prints, each at least 2" square
• 1/4 yard yellow
• 1/8 yard muslin
• 1/8 yard green print
• 11" x 14" piece of backing fabric
• 11" x 14" piece of thin batting

CUTTING

All dimensions include a 1/4" seam allowance.
For each of 35 blocks:
• Cut 2: 1" x 2" strips, same scrap
Also:
• Cut 35: 1" x 2" strips, yellow
• Cut 2: 3/4" x 11" strips, yellow, for the border
• Cut 2: 3/4" x 8 1/2" strips, yellow, for the border
• Cut 140: 1" squares, muslin
• Cut 2: 1 3/4" x 25" strips, green print, for the binding

DIRECTIONS

• Draw a diagonal line from corner to corner on the wrong side of each 1" muslin square.

• Place a muslin square on a 1" x 2" print strip, right sides together, aligning the left edges, as shown.

• Stitch on the drawn line. Press the seam allowance toward the print fabric and trim it to 1/8".
• Place a muslin square on the opposite end of the rectangle, lining up the right edges. Stitch on the drawn line, as shown. Press and trim, as before, to complete a pieced strip. Make 70.

• Stitch a 1" x 2" yellow strip between 2 matching pieced strips to complete a block. Make 35.

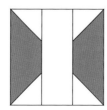

• Lay out the blocks in 7 rows of 5, as shown.

• Stitch the blocks into rows. Join the rows.
• Stitch the 3/4" x 11" yellow strips to the long sides of the quilt.
• Stitch the 3/4" x 8 1/2" yellow strips to the remaining sides of the quilt.
• Finish according to *Mini Stitching Tips*, using the 1 3/4" x 25" green print strips for the binding.

Pinwheels and Posies

The more colors the merrier, when set against solid yellow.

It will be springtime in your home everyday of the year when you make Jeanie Evans' **"Pinwheels and Posies"** (21" x 26 3/4"). The Fort Smith, Arizona, quilter received Honorable Mention in the I998 Miniatures from the Heart Contest with this lively quilt.

QUILT SIZE: 21" x 26 3/4"

MATERIALS
Yardage is estimated for 44" fabric.
- Assorted prints, each at least 1" x 16"
- 2 yards yellow
- 1/4 yard green
- 23" x 29" piece of backing fabric
- 23" x 29" piece of thin batting
- Plastic template material

CUTTING
Pattern piece A is full size and includes a 1/4" seam allowance. Trace pattern piece A onto the plastic template material and cut it out. Mark the seam line on template A according to the pattern piece. Pattern piece D is full size and includes a 1/8" turn-under allowance. Appliqué pattern pieces B and C are full size and do not include a seam allowance. Make a template of the remaining pattern pieces. Trace around templates B and C on the right side of the fabric and add a 1/8" seam

allowance when cutting the pieces out. All other dimensions include a 1/4" seam allowance.
- Cut 63: 1" x 16" strips, assorted prints
- Cut 11: 1" x 6" strips, assorted prints
- Cut 24: B, assorted prints
- Cut 24: D, assorted prints
- Cut 63: 1 1/2" x 16" strips, yellow
- Cut 11: 1 1/2" x 6" strips, yellow
- Cut 4: 2 1/2" x 24" strips, yellow
- Cut 2: 3/4" x 20" strips, green
- Cut 2: 3/4" x 24" strips, green
- Cut 48: C, green
- Cut 3: 1 3/4" x 44" strips, yellow, for the binding

DIRECTIONS
- Stitch a 1 1/2" x 16" yellow strip to a 1" x 16" print strip, right sides together along their length, to form a pieced strip. Press the seam allowance toward the print. Make 63.
- Aligning the marked line on template A with the center seam line of a pieced strip, as shown, cut 6 triangles from the

pieced strip. NOTE: *Do not alternate the direction of the template.*

- Repeat with 55 more pieced strips.
- Join 3 matching pieced triangles to make a Half-block, as shown. Make 2.

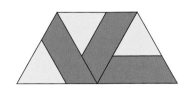

- In the same manner, make 55 more sets of 2 matching Half-blocks.
- Cut 5 matching A's from each of the remaining 16"-long pieced strips. From them, make 7 more Half-blocks to fill in the top and bottom edges of the quilt. You will have 2 A's left over from each

pieced strip to use along the side edges of the quilt.

• Stitch a 1 1/2" x 6" yellow strip to a 1" x 6" print strip, right sides together along their length, to form a pieced strip. Press the seam allowance toward the print. Make 11.

• Aligning the template as before, cut 2 A's from each 6"-long pieced strip to use along the side edges of the quilt.

• Referring to the Assembly Diagram, lay out the Half-blocks and pieced triangles in horizontal rows. Match pairs of Half-blocks in the layout so they'll form whole blocks. Match pieced triangles in pairs along the edges and place a single pieced triangle in each of the bottom corners.

• Stitch the Half-blocks and pieced triangles into horizontal rows. Join the rows.

• Trim the long sides of the quilt 1/4" beyond the outermost points of the whole blocks as indicated by the dashed lines.

• Measure the length of the quilt. Trim two 2 1/2" x 24" yellow strips to that measurement. Stitch them to the long sides of the quilt.

• Measure the width of the quilt, including the borders. Trim the remaining 2 1/2" x 24" yellow strips to that measurement. Stitch them to the remaining sides of the quilt.

• Press under a 1/4" seam allowance along both long edges of the green strips.

• Center the two 24"-long green strips on the long side borders and pin them in place. Center the two 20"-long green strips on the short borders and pin them in place.

• Place a print B in each corner, covering the intersection of the green strips. Trim any excess from the green strips before appliquéing the corner B's in place.

• Evenly space 6 B's along each long border and 4 B's along each short border. Appliqué them in place over the green strips.

• Appliqué the green strips in place between the B's.

• Referring to the quilt photo as needed, appliqué 2 C's between each pair of B's.

• Fold 1/8" of the raw edge of a print D toward the wrong side. Thread a needle with a single strand of quilting thread.

Leaving 2" tail of thread, stitch around the circle with a short running stitch close to the fold, as shown.

• Pull the ends of the thread tightly to gather a fabric circle and form a yo-yo. Tie off the thread inside of the yo-yo to secure it. Make 24.

• Slipstitch a yo-yo to the center of each print B.

• Finish according to *Mini Stitching Tips,* using the 1 3/4" x 44" yellow strips for the binding.

ASSEMBLY DIAGRAM

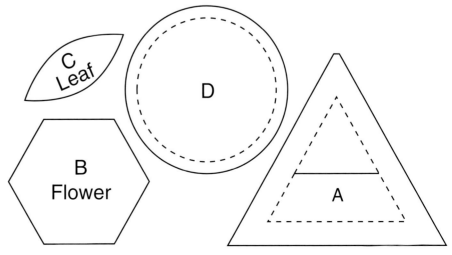

Scotties in the Corners

Animals and clowns frolic within these pinwheels.

After seeing the 1930's collection of red, black and white prints by Maywood Studio, I couldn't resist making **"Scotties in the Corners"** (9" square). You might enjoy stitching a gay little quilt like this to decorate a young child's bedroom.

QUILT SIZE: 9" square
BLOCK SIZE: 2" square

MATERIALS

Yardage is estimated for 44" fabric.
- Assorted reds and red prints, each at least 2 1/4" square
- Assorted black prints, each at least 2" square
- Fat eighth (11" x 18") black
- Fat eighth muslin
- Fat eighth burgundy
- Scraps of Scottie print (or other novelty print)
- Fat eighth black polka dot
- 11" square of backing fabric
- 11" square of thin batting

CUTTING

Dimensions include a 1/4" seam allowance. Trim seams to 1/8" after stitching and pressing.
- Cut 9: 2 3/4" squares, assorted reds and red prints
- Cut 9: 2 3/4" squares, muslin
- Cut 4: 1 7/8" squares, assorted black prints
- Cut 14: 1 7/8" squares, black
- Cut 2: 3/4" x 7" strips, black
- Cut 8: 3/4" x 6 1/2" strips, burgundy
- Cut 1: 1 1/4" x 7" strip, burgundy
- Cut 8: 3/4" x 1 1/4" strips, burgundy
- Cut 4: 1 1/4" squares, scottie print, centering the motif in the square
- Cut 4: 1 1/4" x 6 1/2" strips, black polka dot

- Cut 3: 1 3/4" x 18" strips, black, for the binding

DIRECTIONS
- Draw a diagonal line from corner to corner on the wrong side of each 2 3/4" muslin square.
- Lay a marked muslin square on a 2 3/4" red or red print square, right sides together. Stitch 1/4" away from the diagonal line on both sides, as shown. Make 9.
- Cut the squares apart on the marked line to yield 18 pieced squares.
- Mark a diagonal line from corner to corner on the wrong side of each 1 7/8" black or black print square.
- Lay a marked square on a pieced square, right sides together, with the marked line perpendicular to the seam of the pieced square.
- Stitch 1/4" away from the marked line on both sides, as before. Make 18. Cut the squares apart on the marked line to yield 36 pieced units.

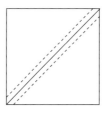

- Stitch 4 pieced units together to complete a block. Make 9. NOTE: *Some blocks will spin in one direction and the rest will spin in the opposite direction.*

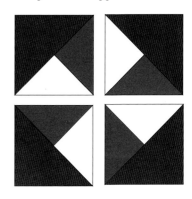

- Referring to the photo as needed, lay out the blocks in 3 rows of 3. Stitch the blocks into rows and join the rows.
- Stitch a 3/4" x 1 1/4" burgundy strip to the top and bottom of each 1 1/4" Scottie print square. Set them aside.

- Stitch a 1 1/4" x 7" burgundy strip between two 3/4" x 7" black strips, along their length.
- Cut eight 3/4" slices from the pieced strip.

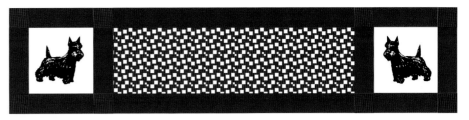

- Stitch a slice to opposite sides of each Scottie print unit to complete a Nine Patch unit. Make 4. Set them aside.
- Stitch a 1 1/4" x 6 1/2" black polka dot strip between two 3/4" x 6 1/2" burgundy strips, along their length, to form a pieced border strip. Make 4.

- Stitch 2 of the pieced border strips to opposite sides of the quilt.
- Stitch a Nine Patch unit to each short end of a pieced border strip. Make 2.
- Stitch them to the top and bottom of the quilt.

- Finish according to *Mini Stitching Tips,* using the 1 3/4" x 18" black strips for the binding.

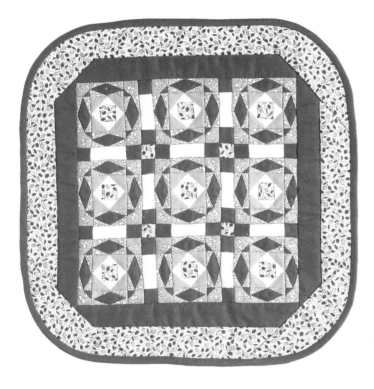

Storm at Sea

The smallest of blocks are manageable with foundation piecing.

The inspiration for this little **"Storm at Sea"** (11 3/4" square) came from a description, published in *Traditional Quiltworks* magazine, of a full-size antique quilt. Even the tiniest pieces are easy to handle with foundation piecing. I chose reproduction fabric in various shades of purple, but you can choose prints and solids in your favorite color to make a mini that really creates a stir.

QUILT SIZE: 11 3/4" square
BLOCK SIZE: 2 1/4" square

MATERIALS
Yardage is estimated for 44" fabric.
- 1/2 yard dark purple
- Fat eighth (11" x 18") light purple
- Fat eighth muslin
- Fat eighth medium purple print
- Fat eighth light floral
- 14" square of backing fabric
- 14" square of thin batting
- Paper for the foundations

CUTTING
Dimensions include a 1/4" seam allowance. Fabrics for foundation piec-ing will be cut as you sew the blocks. Each piece must be at least 1/4" larger on all sides than the section it will cover. Refer to Mini Stitching Tips *as needed.*
- Cut 4: 1" squares, light floral
- Cut 2: 1 1/2" x 9 3/4" strips, light floral
- Cut 2: 1 1/2" x 11 3/4" strips, light floral
- Cut 2: 4 1/2" squares, light floral, then cut them in half diagonally to yield 4 triangles
- Cut 1: 1 3/4" x 13" strip, muslin
- Cut 2: 1" x 13" strips, dark purple
- Cut 2: 1 1/4" x 8 1/4" strips, dark purple
- Cut 2: 1 1/4" x 9 3/4" strips, dark pur-ple
- Cut 3: 1 3/4" x 18" bias strips, dark purple, for the binding

DIRECTIONS
Follow the foundation piecing instruc-tions in Mini Stitching Tips *to piece the units. Trace the full-size patterns on the foundation material, transferring all lines and numbers and leaving a 1" space between foundations. Make 9 of Foundation A, 36 of Foundation B and 36 of Foundation C. Cut each one out 1/2" beyond the broken line.*
For each Foundation A:
- Use the following fabrics in these positions:

1 - light floral
2,3,4,5 - muslin
6,7,8,9 - light purple

For each Foundation B:
• Use the following fabrics in these positions:
    1 - dark purple
    2, 3, 4, 5 - medium purple print
For each Foundation C:
• Use the following fabrics in these positions:
    1 - medium purple print
    2, 3, 4 - light purple
    5 - dark purple
• Baste each foundation in the seam allowance, halfway between the stitching line and the broken line, to hold the fabrics in place, if desired.
• Trim each foundation on the broken line.
• Lay out a Foundation A, 4 Foundation B's and 4 Foundation C's, as shown.

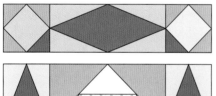

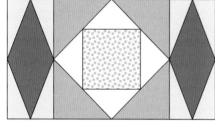

• Stitch the foundations into rows and join the rows to complete a block. Make 9.
• Stitch a 1 3/4" x 13" muslin strip between two 1" x 13" dark purple strips, along their length.
• Cut twelve 1" slices from the pieced strip.

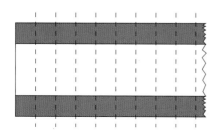

• Stitch 3 blocks and 2 slices together, as shown, to complete a row. Make 3.

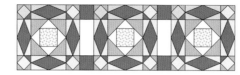

• Stitch 3 slices and two 1" light floral squares together, as shown, to complete a sashing row. Make 2.

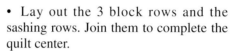

• Lay out the 3 block rows and the sashing rows. Join them to complete the quilt center.
• Stitch the 1 1/4" x 8 1/4" dark purple strips to opposite sides of the quilt.
• Stitch the 1 1/4" x 9 3/4" dark purple strips to the remaining sides of the quilt.
• In the same manner, stitch the 1 1/2" x 9 3/4" light floral strips to opposite sides of the quilt.
• Stitch the 1 1/2" x 11 3/4" light floral strips to the remaining sides of the quilt.
• Working with one corner of the quilt, place the 1 1/2" mark of a ruler along the Foundation A seam between the muslin and the light purple triangle. Trim the corner of the quilt along the edge of the ruler. Repeat for the remaining 3 corners.

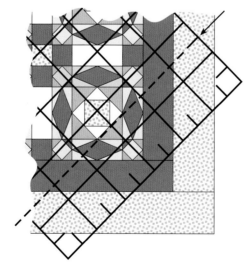

• Center and stitch a light floral triangle to each corner. Trim to square each corner.

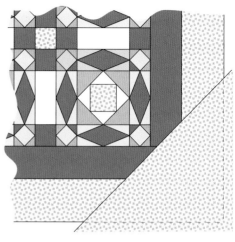

• Remove the paper foundations now.
• Mark a curve at each corner of the quilt top. Cut the quilt on the curved line.
• Finish according to *Mini Stitching Tips*, using the 1 3/4" x 18" dark purple bias strips for the binding.

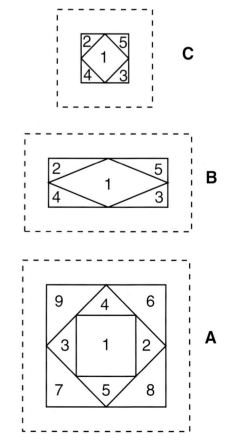

Thirties Four-Patch

A wide selection of prints and solids enlivens the simplest of blocks.

Mary K. Richmond of Santa Maria, California, intended to use up the scraps from her collection of solids and reproduction prints when she made "**Thirties Four-Patch**" (33" square). What she learned, though, was that no matter how many blocks she pieced, the pile of scraps seemed to keep growing.

QUILT SIZE: 33" square
BLOCK SIZE: 3" square

MATERIALS
Yardage is estimated for 44" fabric.
• Assorted medium to dark print scraps totaling at least 1/2 yard
• Assorted medium to dark solid scraps, each at least 1 1/4" x 6"
• 1/8 yard pink print
• 1/8 yard blue print
• 1/8 yard yellow print
• 1/8 yard green print
• 1/4 yard white
• 1/4 yard pink
• 1/4 yard blue
• 1/4 yard yellow
• 1/4 yard green
• 35" square of backing fabric
• 35" square of thin batting

CUTTING
Dimensions include a 1/4" seam allowance.
For each of 32 Four-Patch blocks:
• Cut 1: 1 1/4" x 6" strip, solid
• Cut 2: 2" squares, same color print
Also:
• Cut 32: 3 1/2" squares, assorted prints
• Cut 32: 1 1/4" x 6" strips, white
• Cut 4: 1 1/4" x 35" strips, white
• Cut 1: 4" x 35" strip, pink
• Cut 1: 4" x 35" strip, blue
• Cut 1: 4" x 35" strip, yellow
• Cut 1: 4" x 35" strip, green
• Cut 1: 1 3/4" x 44" strip each from

the pink, blue, yellow and green prints, for the binding

DIRECTIONS
For each of the Four-Patch blocks:
• Stitch a 1 1/4" x 6" solid strip to a 1 1/4" x 6" white strip, right sides together along their length. Press the seam allowance toward the solid strip.
• Cut four 1 1/4" slices from the pieced strip.

• Stitch 2 slices together to complete a Four-patch unit. Make 2.
• Lay out the 2 Four-patch units and two 2" print squares. Stitch them together to complete a Four-Patch block.

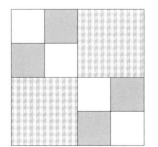

ASSEMBLY
• Referring to the quilt photo as needed, lay out 8 rows of 8 blocks, alternating the pieced blocks with 3 1/2" print

squares.
• Stitch the blocks into rows and join the rows.
• Stitch a 1 1/4" x 35" white strip to a 4" x 35" pink strip, right sides together, along their length, to form a pieced border. In the same manner, stitch a 1 1/4" x 35" white strip to each of the remaining 4" x 35" blue, yellow and green strips.
• Center and stitch the pink and yellow borders to opposite sides of the quilt, keeping the white strip against the quilt center. Start, stop and backstitch 1/4" from the each edge.
• Center and stitch the blue and green borders to the remaining sides of the quilt in the same manner. Miter each corner, referring to *Mini Stitching Tips* as needed.
• Finish according to *Mini Stitching Tips*, but do not join the binding strips to form a single length. After folding the binding strips in half lengthwise, wrong sides together, and pressing, measure the quilt and trim the blue and green print binding strips to that measurement. Stitch the blue and green print binding to the edge of the matching blue and green borders. Measure the quilt including the blue and green print bindings. Add 1/2" to that measurement. Trim the pink and yellow print binding strips to that measurement and stitch them to the matching pink and yellow borders turning the ends under 1/4".

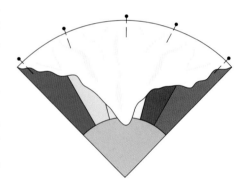

Fans

Foundation-pieced fans you can make in a breeze!

E. Helen Codd made the adorable blocks in **"Fans"** (13" x 15") from 1930s vintage prints. Helen, who is from Poole, Dorset, England, used fabric scraps, sent by an American friend who restores quilts, for her "fantastic" miniature.

QUILT SIZE: 13" x 15"
BLOCK SIZE: 2" square

MATERIALS

Yardage is estimated for 44" fabric.
- Assorted print scraps, each at least 1" x 1 3/4"
- 1/2 yard white
- Fat eighth (11" x 18") blue print
- 15" x 17" piece of backing fabric
- 15" x 17" piece of thin batting
- Paper for the foundations

CUTTING

Fabric for foundation piecing the fan unit will be cut as you sew the blocks. Each piece should be at least 1/2" larger on all sides than the section it will cover. *Pattern Piece A will be appliquéd and has a 1/4" seam allowance on the straight sides and a 1/4" turn-under allowance on the curved side. Refer to* Mini Stitching Tips *as needed. All other dimensions include a 1/4" seam allowance.*
- Cut 30: A, blue print
- Cut 4: 1 3/4" x 17" blue print strips, for the borders
- Cut 3: 1 3/4" x 25" bias strips, white, for the binding
- Cut 30: B, white

DIRECTIONS

Follow the foundation piecing instructions in Mini Stitching Tips *to piece the fan units.*
- Trace the full-size fan pattern 30 times on the foundation material, transferring all lines and numbers and leaving a 1" space between foundations. Cut each one out 1/2" beyond the broken line.
- Piece each fan foundation in numerical order, using a print in each fan blade position. Make 30.
- Press the curved side of a blue print A under 1/4" and trim to 1/8" to reduce bulk.
- Mark the center of the curved side of an A with a pin.
- Center and pin the A in several places to the center of the inner curve of the fan blades, as shown, being sure the outer edges are lined up.

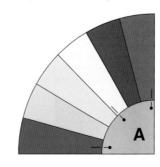

- Appliqué the A to the fan blades, being careful not to catch the paper foundation in your stitches. Make 30.
- Mark the center of the curved side of a white B with a pin.

- Center and pin the B in several places to the outer curved edge of the fan blades.

- Stitch the B to the fan blades. Make 30.
- Remove the paper foundations now.
- Lay out the Fan blocks in 6 rows of 5. Stitch the blocks into rows and join the rows.
- Center and stitch a 1 3/4" x 17" blue print strip to each side of the quilt. Start, stop and backstitch 1/4" from each edge.
- Miter each corner referring to *Mini Stitching Tips* as needed.
- Mark a curve at each corner of the quilt top. Cut the quilt on the curved line.
- Finish according to *Mini Stitching Tips*, using the 1 3/4" x 25" white bias strips for the binding.

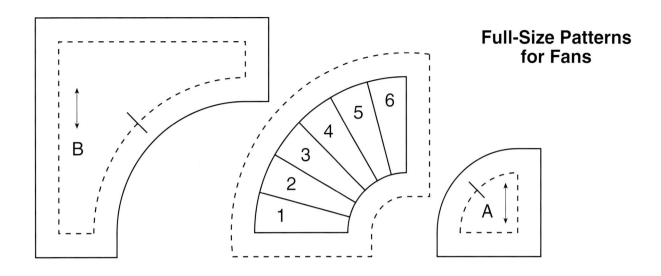

**Full-Size Patterns
for Fans**

Butterflies

Design by Nancy Ward Castonia

*Take wing while foundation
piecing spring butterflies!*

Fabrics from the 1930s and a traditional pattern from the same time period give Nancy Ward Castonia's **"Butterflies"** (11 1/4" square) an antique look. The quilter from Cumberland, Maine, selected these fabrics because butterflies were a popular design during the Depression era.

QUILT SIZE: 11 1/4" square
BLOCKS SIZE: 2 1/2" square

MATERIALS
Yardage is estimated for 44" fabric.
• Assorted scraps of pink, purple, blue and yellow prints
• Fat eighth (11" x 18") yellow
• Fat eighth pink
• 1/4 yard green
• 14" square of backing fabric
• 14" square of thin batting
• Paper for the foundations

CUTTING
Dimensions include a 1/4" seam allowance. Fabric for foundation piecing will be cut as you sew the blocks. Each piece should be at least 1/2" larg- er on all sides than the section it will cover. Refer to *Mini Stitching Tips as needed.*
• Cut 2: 3/4" x 3" strips, pink, for the sashing
• Cut 3: 3/4" x 5 3/4" strips, pink, for the sashing
• Cut 2: 3/4" x 6 1/4" strips, pink, for the sashing
• Cut 2: 3" x 6 1/4" strips, green, for the border
• Cut 2: 3" x 11 1/4" strips, green, for the border
• Cut 2: 1 3/4" x 44" strips, green, for the binding

DIRECTIONS
Follow the foundation piecing instruction in Mini Stitching Tips *to piece the* blocks.
• Trace each unit 4 times on the foundation material, transferring all lines and numbers and leaving a 1" space between foundations. Cut each one out 1/2" beyond the broken line.
NOTE: *Each block will consist of an A and B unit. Choose 3 different prints for each Butterfly block.*
For Unit A:
• Use the following fabrics in these positions:
　　1 - first print
　　2 - yellow
　　3 - second print
　　4 - yellow
　　5 - third print
　　6 - second print
　　7 - yellow

For Unit B:
- Use the following fabrics in these positions:
  - 1 - second print
  - 2 - yellow
  - 3 - third print
  - 4 - second print
  - 5, 6 - yellow
- Baste each unit in the seam allowance, halfway between the stitching line and the broken line, to hold the fabrics in place, if desired.
- Trim each unit on the broken line.
- Stitch matching A and B units together to make a Butterfly block. Make 4.

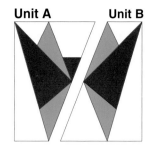

Unit A   Unit B

- Lay out the Butterfly blocks and the pink sashing strips according to the Assembly Diagram.

- Stitch the 3/4" x 3" sashing strips and blocks into horizontal rows.
- Join the rows and the 3/4" x 5 3/4" sashing strips.
- Stitch the 3/4" x 6 1/4" sashing strips to the sides of the quilt.
- Stitch the 3" x 6 1/4" green strips to the top and bottom of the quilt.
- Stitch the 3" x 11 1/4" green strips to the sides of the quilt.
- Remove the paper foundations now.
- Finish according to *Mini Stitching Tips,* using the 1 3/4" x 44" green strips for the binding.

ASSEMBLY DIAGRAM

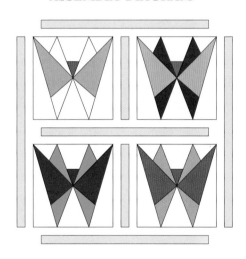

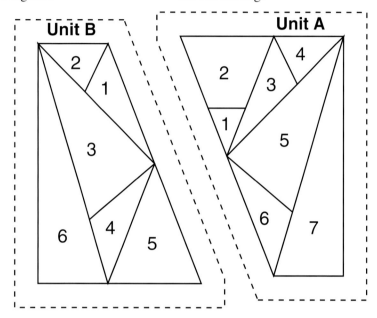

Rainbow Cabins

Stabilize quarter-inch logs with foundation piecing.

Judy Randel of Woodland, California, used 1930s reproduction prints in every possible color to make **"Rainbow Cabins"** (9 1/4" x 12 3/4").

QUILT SIZE: 9 1/4" x 12 3/4"
BLOCK SIZE: 1 3/4" square

MATERIALS
Yardage is estimated for 44" fabric.
- Assorted prints in red, pink, peach, yellow, green, blue and purple
- Fat eighth (11" x 18") pink

print
- 12" x 15" piece of backing fabric
- 12" x 15" piece of thin batting
- Paper for the foundations

CUTTING
Dimensions include a 1/4" seam allowance. Fabric for foundation piecing will be cut as you sew the

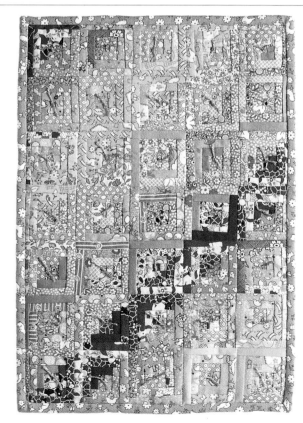

blocks. Each piece must be at least 1/4" larger on all sides than the section it will cover. Refer to Mini Stitching Tips as needed.
• Cut 4: 1 3/4" x 18" strips, pink print, for the binding

DIRECTIONS
Follow the foundation piecing instructions in Mini Stitching Tips *to piece the blocks.*
• Trace the full-size pattern 35 times on the foundation material, transferring all lines and numbers and leaving a 1" space between foundations. Cut each one out 1/2" beyond the broken line.

For each of 5 Red/Pink blocks:
• Use the following fabrics in these positions:
 1 - red print
 2, 3 - pink print
 4, 5 - red print
 6, 7 - pink print
 8, 9 - red print
 10, 11 - pink print
 12, 13 - red print

For each of 5 Pink/Peach blocks:
• Use the following fabrics in these positions:
 1 - pink print
 2, 3 - peach print
 4, 5 - pink print
 6, 7 - peach print
 8, 9 - pink print
 10, 11 - peach print
 12, 13 - pink print

For each of 5 Peach/Yellow blocks:
• Use the following fabrics in these positions:

 1 - peach print
 2, 3 - yellow print
 4, 5 - peach print
 6, 7 - yellow print
 8, 9 - peach print
 10, 11 - yellow print
 12, 13 - peach print

For each of 5 Yellow/Green blocks:
• Use the following fabrics in these positions:
 1 - yellow print
 2, 3 - green print
 4, 5 - yellow print
 6, 7 - green print
 8, 9 - yellow print
 10, 11 - green print
 12, 13 - yellow print

For each of 5 Green/Blue blocks:
• Use the following fabrics in these positions:
 1 - green print
 2, 3 - blue print
 4, 5 - green print
 6, 7 - blue print
 8, 9 - green print
 10, 11 - blue print
 12, 13 - green print

For each of 5 Blue/Purple blocks:
• Use the following fabrics in these positions:
 1 - blue print
 2, 3 - purple print
 4, 5 - blue print
 6, 7 - purple print
 8, 9 - blue print
 10, 11 - purple print
 12, 13 - blue print

For each of 5 Purple/Red blocks:
• Use the following fabrics in these positions:
 1 - purple print
 2, 3 - red print
 4, 5 - purple print
 6, 7 - red print
 8, 9 - purple print
 10, 11 - red print
 12, 13 - purple print

• Baste each foundation in the seam allowance, halfway between the stitching line and the broken line, to hold the fabrics in place, if desired.
• Trim each foundation on the broken line.
• Referring to the photo, lay out the blocks in 7 rows of 5. Stitch the blocks into rows and join the rows.
• Remove the paper foundations now.
• Finish according to *Mini Stitching Tips,* using the 1 3/4" x 18" pink print strips for the binding.

Full-size Foundation for Rainbow Cabin

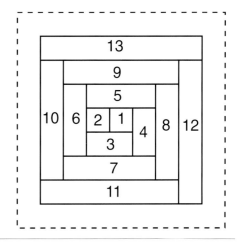

Mom I'll Always Remember, continued from page 9

Quotes from mom...

• Yes I do have eyes in the back of my head.
• Why didn't you go before we left home?
• When you buy the food in this house, you can have pizza every day.
• Don't yell I'm not deaf.
• I wasn't born yesterday.
• Don't sit so close to the TV, it's bad for your eyes.
• If you're trying to drive me crazy, you're too late.

• Just wait until your dad gets home.
• Don't tell me it's not your turn.
• Were you born in a barn?
• You'd take my underwear if they'd fit you.
• OK, go ahead and live like a pig, see if I care.
• Because I said so.
• Just wait until you have kids of your own.

• And when they turn out just like you, you'll know how I've suffered.
• I didn't get this gray hair at the beauty parlor.
• Act your age not your shoe size.
• Your dad says you can't get up until you eat these porcupine meatballs.
• What happened to the floor? I can't find it.
• I love you.

Baby Bear

Add a three dimensional element with prairie points.

"Baby Bear" (12 1/2" square), by Kris Porter of Wichita, Kansas, was born of leftovers from a king-size quilt. Kris put the tiny triangles; trimmed from speed-pieced triangles in her larger quilt, to good use in this miniature.

QUILT SIZE: 12 1/2" square
BLOCK SIZE: 3 1/2" square

MATERIALS
Yardage is estimated for 44" fabric.
• Assorted prints totaling at least 1/2 yard
• Fat eighth (11" x 18") black
• 1/2 yard white
• 15" square of backing fabric
• 15" square of thin batting

CUTTING
Dimensions include a 1/4" seam allowance.
• Cut 48: 1 1/2" squares, assorted prints
• Cut 4: 1" squares, gold print
• Cut 32: 1 3/8" squares, assorted prints
• Cut 48: 2" squares, assorted prints
• Cut 8: 1" x 2" strips, assorted prints
• Cut 32: 1 3/8" squares, white
• Cut 16: 1" x 2" strips, white
• Cut 2: 1" x 4" strips, white
• Cut 1: 1" x 8" strip, white
• Cut 16: 1" squares, white
• Cut 16: 1 1/2" x 2 1/2" strips, white
• Cut 4: 1 1/2" squares, white
• Cut 4: 1" x 8 1/2" strips, white
• Cut 2: 3/4" x 8" strips, black
• Cut 2: 3/4" x 9" strips, black

PIECING
• Draw a diagonal line from corner to corner on the wrong side of each 1 3/8" white square.
• Lay a marked white square on a 1 3/8" print square, right sides together. Stitch 1/4" away from the

diagonal line on both sides. Make 32. Cut the squares apart on the marked line to yield 64 pieced squares.
• Stitch 2 pieced squares together to form a pieced unit, as shown. Mixing the prints at random, make 16 pieced units.

• Stitch 2 pieced squares together to form a reverse unit, as shown. Mixing the prints as before, make 16 reverse units.
• Stitch a 1" white square to one end of a reverse unit to make a pieced row, as shown. Make 16.
• Lay out a pieced unit, a pieced row and a 1 1/2" print square. Join the pieces to complete a paw unit. Make 16.
• Lay out 4 paw units, alternating directions and placing 1" x 2" white strips between the units. Sew the units and strips together to complete a paw row. Make 4.

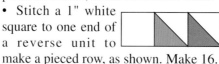

• Lay out two 1" x 2" white strips, a 1" x 4" white strip and two 1" gold print squares, end to end, as shown. Join them to form a pieced sashing. Make 2.

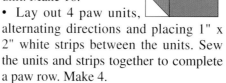

• Referring to the quilt photo as needed, lay out the 4 block rows, 2 pieced sashings and the 1" x 8" white strip. Join the rows, sashings and strip to complete the quilt center.

• Stitch the 3/4" x 8" black strips to opposite sides of the quilt.
• Stitch the 3/4" x 9" black strips to the remaining sides of the quilt.
• Draw a diagonal line, from corner to corner, on the wrong side of each remaining 1 1/2" print square.
• Lay a marked print square on a 1 1/2" x 2 1/2" white strip, right sides together, and stitch along the diagonal line.

• Trim 1/4" beyond the seam. Open the unit and press the seam allowance toward the print.
• Lay a marked print square on the other end of the white strip, as shown, and stitch

along the diagonal line. Trim and press as before to complete a Flying Geese unit. Make 16.
• Stitch 4 Flying Geese units together, end to end, to form a pieced border. Make 4.

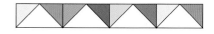

• Fold a 2" print square in half, wrong sides together, and press. Place it on the work surface with the fold at the top.
• Bring one top corner down until it meets the mid-point and raw edges are aligned, as shown.

• In the same manner, bring the other corner down to form a triangle and complete a prairie

point, as shown.
- Press the folds. Baste along the raw edges, if desired. Make 48 prairie points.
- Center and pin a prairie point, center fold up, on each of the Flying Geese units in the pieced borders. Baste in place.

- Stitch pieced borders, with the prairie points, to two opposite sides of the quilt.
- Stitch 1 1/2" white squares to both ends of the remaining pieced borders.
- Stitch them to the remaining sides of the quilt.
- Sew a 1" x 2" print strip to each end of a 1" x 8 1/2" white strip to form an outer border. Make 4.
- Center and stitch the outer borders to the sides of the quilt top. Start, stop and backstitch 1/4" from each edge.
- Miter each corner, referring to *Mini Stitching Tips*, as needed.
- Layer and baste the quilt, referring to *Mini Stitching Tips*. Quilt as desired, leaving the outer border unquilted for now. Trim the batting even with the edge of the quilt top, but do not trim the backing yet.
- Place 8 prairie points along the edge of each side of the quilt, keeping the points toward the center of the quilt, the center fold facing down and raw edges aligned. Pin them in place.

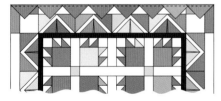

- Stitch them to the quilt top and batting with a 1/4" seam allowance, keeping the backing out of the way.
- Turn the points away from the quilt and lightly press the seam allowances to the back. Trim the batting in the seam allowance to reduce bulk, if desired.
- Trim the backing 1/2" beyond the edge of the quilt top.
- Fold 1/2" of the backing to the wrong side and slipstich the folded edge to the wrong side of the prairie points along the stitching line.
- Finish quilting the outer border, as desired.

Mini Stitching Tips

Fabric Selection

We recommend 100% cotton for most projects because it is easy to finger press and handles nicely. The yardage requirements in our patterns are based on a standard 44" wide bolt. However, many of the quilts can be made from assorted scraps.

Fabric Preparation

We suggest washing fabrics before using them in your minis. Test all fabrics to be sure they are colorfast.

Templates

Trace pattern pieces on clear plastic. Use a permanent marker to list the name of the block, total number of pieces, pattern letter and grainline on each template.

Pieced Patterns

Unless otherwise noted, patterns include 1/4" seam allowances. For smaller units, we suggest trimming the seam allowance to 1/8" after stitching and pressing, to reduce bulk. The solid line is the cutting line and the broken line is the sewing line. For machine piecing, make the template with the seam allowance. Trace around the template on the right side of the fabric. For hand piecing, make the template without the seam allowance. Trace the template on the wrong side of the fabric and add a 1/4" seam allowance as you cut.

Foundation-pieced Patterns

Foundation piecing is a method for making even the smallest blocks with a high degree of accuracy. For each foundation, trace all of the lines and numbers onto paper. You will need one foundation for each block or part of a block. The solid line is the stitching line and the broken line is the cutting line. The fabric pieces you select do not have to be cut precisely. Be generous when cutting fabric pieces as excess fabric will be trimmed away after sewing. Your goal is to cut a piece that covers the numbered area and extends into surrounding areas after seams are stitched. Generally, fabric pieces should be large enough to extend 1/2" beyond the seamline on all sides before stitching. For very small sections, or sections without angles, 1/4" may be sufficient. Select a short stitch length, 12-14 stitches per inch.

Place fabric pieces on the unmarked side of the foundation and stitch on the marked side. Center the first piece, right side up, over section 1 on the unmarked side of the foundation. Hold the foundation up to a light to make sure that the raw edges of the fabric extend at least 1/2" beyond the seamline on all sides. Hold this first piece in place with a small dab of glue or a pin, if desired. Place the fabric for section 2 on the first piece, right sides together. Turn the foundation over and sew on the line between 1 and 2, extending the stitching past the beginning and end of the line by a few stitches on both ends. Trim the seam allowance to 1/8". Fold the section 2 piece back, right side up and press. Continue adding pieces to the foundation in the same manner until all sections are covered and the block is complete.

Unless instructed to do otherwise, do not remove the paper until the blocks have been joined together and at least one border has been added, to avoid disturbing the stitches. Use tweezers to carefully remove sections of the paper. The pieces will be perforated from the stitching and can be gently pulled free.

Appliqué Patterns

Unless otherwise indicated, a seam allowance is not included on appliqué pieces. The solid line is the sewing line. Make a template and lightly trace around it on the right side of the fabric. Then "eyeball" a 1/8" to 3/16" turn-under allowance when cutting the fabric. Clip inside curves almost to the pencil line so they will turn under smoothly as you stitch.

Marking Fabric

We suggest using silver or white marking tools for dark fabrics and fine line pencils for light fabrics. Always use a sharp pencil and a light touch. Lay a piece of fine-grained sandpaper under the fabric to keep it from slipping while you mark it.

Hand Sewing

Use a thin, short needle ("sharp") to ensure a flat seam. Sew only on the marked sewing line using small, even stitches.

Needleturn Appliqué

Pin an appliqué piece in position on the background fabric. Using thread to match the appliqué piece, thread a needle with a 15" to 18" length and knot one end. Turn under the allowance and bring the needle from the wrong side of the background fabric up through the fold on the marked line of the appliqué piece. Push the needle through the background fabric, catching a

Mini Stitching Tips

few threads, and come back up through the appliqué piece on the marked line close to the first stitch. Use the point of the needle to smooth under the allowance and make another stitch in the same way. Continue needleturning and stitching until the piece is completely sewn to the background fabric. To reduce bulk, do not stitch where one appliqué piece will be overlapped by another.

Machine Sewing

Set the stitch length to 14 stitches per inch. Cut a length of masking tape or moleskin foot pad about 1/4" x 2". Place a clear plastic ruler under and to the left of the needle aligning the right edge of the ruler 1/4" from the point of the needle along the throat plate. Stick the masking tape or moleskin in place at the ruler's edge. Feed fabric under the needle, touching this guide.

Pressing

Generally, seams are pressed toward the darker of the two fabrics. Press abutting seams in opposite directions whenever possible. Use a dry iron and press carefully, as little blocks are easy to distort. You may want to press seams open, to reduce bulk, in small units.

Making Bias Strips

Most miniature work requires bias strips of 25" or less. Unless instructed to use a different size in the pattern, begin with an 18" fabric square. Lay your clear plastic ruler diagonally across the square and cut from corner to corner. Cut a bias strip the width you require, measuring from the diagonal cut. This strip will be 25". Additional diagonal cuts will decrease in length. Cut as many as required for your pattern.

FINISHING
Marking

Cut simple designs from clear plastic adhesive-backed shelf paper. They'll stick and re-stick long enough to finish the quilt. Use masking tape to mark grids. Remove the tape when you're not quilting to avoid leaving a sticky residue. Mark lightly with pencils; thick lines that won't go away really stand out on a small quilt.

Batting

Use a low-loft or very thin batting. Some quilters peel batting into two layers (leaving some loft and good drape); others

use flannel as a filler. Layer the quilt sandwich as follows: backing, wrong side up; batting; quilt top, right side up. Baste or pin the layers together.

Quilting

Very small quilts can be lap-quilted without a hoop. Larger ones can be quilted in a hoop or small frame. Use a short, thin needle ("between") and small stitches that will be in scale with the little quilt. Thread the needle with a single strand of quilting thread and knot one end. Insert the needle through the quilt top and batting (not the backing) an inch away from where you want to begin quilting. Gently pull the thread to pop the knot through the top and bury it in the batting. Too much quilting can flatten a miniature and set the quilt "out of square." Too little quilting causes puffiness which can detract from the scale of the quilt. Experiment and decide what you like best. When the quilting is finished, trim the back and batting even with the top.

Binding

For most straight-edged quilts, a double-fold French binding is an attractive, durable and easy finish. NOTE: *If your quilt has curved or scalloped edges, binding strips must be cut on the bias of the fabric.* To make 1/4" finished binding, cut each strip 1 3/4" wide. Sew binding strips (cross-grain or bias) together with diagonal seams; trim and press seams open.

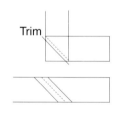

Fold the binding strip in half lengthwise, wrong sides together and press. Position the binding strip on the right side of the quilt top, aligning the raw edges of the binding with the edge of the quilt top. Leave approximately 4" of the binding strip free. Beginning several inches from one corner, stitch the binding to the quilt with a 1/4" seam allowance. When you reach a corner, stop the stitching line exactly 1/4" from the edge. Backstitch, clip threads and remove the quilt from the machine. Fold the binding up and away, creating a 45° angle, as shown.

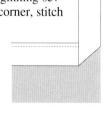

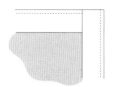

Fold the binding down as shown, and begin stitching at the edge.

Continue stitching around the quilt to within 4" of the starting point. To finish, fold both strips back along the edge of the quilt so that the folded edges meet an equal distance from both lines of stitching and the binding lies flat on the quilt. Finger

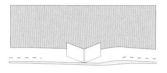

press to crease the folds. Cut both strips 7/8" from the folds.

Open both strips and place the ends at right angles to each other, right sides together. Fold the bulk of the quilt out of your way. Join the strips with a diagonal seam, as shown.

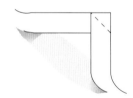

Trim the seam to 1/4" and press it open. Fold the joined strips so that the wrong sides are together again. Place the binding flat against the quilt and finish stitching it to the quilt. Clip the corners. Trim the batting and backing even with the edge of the quilt top so that the binding edge will be filled with batting when you fold the binding to the back of the quilt. Blindstitch the binding to the back of the quilt, covering the seamline.

Sign Your Quilt

Small quilts are revered by collectors, and the little quilts we make today will be treasured by our families and friends. Using embroidery, cross-stitch or permanent marker, write your name and other important data like your city, the date the quilt was completed and for whom the quilt was made somewhere on the back, or attach a label. Someone will be glad you did!